passion for puddings

Shelter

A passion for puddings

Phil Vickery

SIMON & SCHUSTER
A CBS COMPANY

First published in Great Britain by Simon & Schuster UK Ltd 2005

A CBS Company

This edition published 2006

Copyright © 2005 Société Des Produits Nestlé

Simon & Schuster UK Ltd

Africa House

64-68 Kingsway

London

WC2B 6AH

1 3 5 7 9 10 8 6 4 2

Author: Phil Vickery

Design: Simon Daley

Food photography: Steve Baxter

Chocolate Banoffee Pie photograph, page 16: Philip Webb

Home economist: Beatrice Harling

Food stylist: Jane Suthering

Props stylist: Penny Markham

Copy-editor, Proofreader and Indexer: Judith Hannam

Printed and bound in China

ISBN 0 7432 9569 2 pb

ISBN 0 7432 7561 6 hb

Foreword

When asked what 'home' means to any of us, our answer rarely refers to just four walls. Home is where we bring up our family, where we can relax and be ourselves, the place from which we build our lives and fulfil our potential.

When I think of home, I still think of sitting in the kitchen of my parents' farmhouse in Kent. It was here that my mother, a chef, would prepare mouthwatering puddings for her clients, and, if we were lucky, we would get to eat the leftovers.

Memories and activities such as this enrich our lives — yet they are a distant dream for many. Shelter works every day to help families in bad housing or at risk of homelessness, and campaigns to ensure that the next generation of children will have a better start in life.

We can only do this thanks to the support we get from people like Phil Vickery — a chef almost as good as my mum — and thanks to companies such as Carnation, who made this project possible, as well as people such as you who have bought this wonderful book.

I hope you enjoy creating every recipe in it, and that cooking and eating at home makes you appreciate what so many families miss out on. Most of all, I hope that you share my pride in helping to change the lives of families in bad housing across Britain.

Adam Sampson
Director
Shelter

Shelter

Contents

Introduction

My very first memory of Carnation dates back to the early 70s, when I was a young lad growing up in Lancashire. In the summer, we would rush home from school and go straight out into the garden. My mother would always have tea ready. On the table there would be all kinds of goodies – home-made cakes, jugs of juice and tea, and Mrs King's Haymakers Lemonade. Sandwiches would be jam, banana, sugar (yes, sugar) and my mum's favourite – thick slices of bread spread with sticky condensed milk and squished together. Lovely!

Carnation must run in our family, because my grandmother always used it to make ice cream. Hers was a really simple recipe, just condensed milk and fresh cream, blended together then lightly frozen. It was the perfect accompaniment to her home-made wimberry pie, using the tiny wild blueberries painstakingly picked by me and my brothers in The Trough Of Bowland.

When I became a pastry chef, I already knew that this unique ingredient could be used in many different ways. It's simply irreplaceable in all kinds of great puddings, cakes, sweets and ice creams. It makes a wonderfully silky parfait, the classic filling for Banoffee Pie, the easiest Crème Brûlée ever and, my all-time favourite, the world's finest Key Lime Cheesecake

For me, when you discover an ingredient this good, and this versatile, you know you're onto something really special, and that's why I just had to write this book. Whether you're an experienced cook or a complete beginner, you'll find fantastic recipes for every occasion, from classic comfort puds for the family to posh desserts fit for a dinner party. Before you know it, you'll be sharing my passion for puddings too!

Phil Vickery

Comfort cakes
and puds

Hot chocolate fondant puddings

A rich, velvety chocolate pudding really is comfort food at its best. All you need is lashings of thick cream or ice cream . . . or both!

1 Preheat the oven to 200°C, 400°F, Gas Mark 6. Place a large baking sheet in the oven.

2 Grease and base line six 150 ml (¼ pt) Dariole moulds or pudding basins.

3 Beat together the butter and sugar using an electric hand whisk until pale and creamy. Gradually whisk in the condensed milk.

4 Gently whisk in the eggs, a little at a time, followed by the vanilla and coffee. Add the melted chocolate, mix thoroughly, then add the flour and whisk until smooth.

5 Divide the mixture evenly between the moulds and either store in the refrigerator until needed or place onto the hot baking sheet in the oven and bake for 10 minutes. If cooked from chilled, bake for 12 minutes.

6 Immediately run a knife around the edge of the puddings to un-mould, and dust with icing sugar. I like to serve them with lightly whipped double cream or vanilla ice cream.

Serves 6
Preparation time: 15 minutes
Cooking time: 10 minutes

50 g (2 oz) butter
75 g (3 oz) caster sugar
170 g tube Carnation
    Condensed Milk
4 large eggs, beaten with
    a pinch of salt
1 tsp vanilla extract
1 tbsp Nescafé Espresso coffee
    powder, dissolved in 1 tbsp
    boiling water
350 g (12 oz) dark chocolate, melted
75 g (3 oz) plain or Italian 00 flour
icing sugar, sifted, to dust

Fudgy chocolate croissant pudding

This dessert is the perfect combination of two of my favourite things, Bread and Butter Pudding and Baked Egg Custard. I have always hated waste, and when working in a hotel some years ago I was appalled at how many croissants were thrown away after breakfast. I invented this pudding to use up all the leftovers – it's fab!

1 Grease a 2.4 litre (4¼ pt) ovenproof pudding dish.

2 Cut each croissant into three and arrange in the dish. Place the chocolate in a saucepan with the milk, cream and nutmeg and heat gently until the chocolate has melted.

3 In a large bowl, whisk together the egg yolks and the condensed milk, then gradually beat in the hot chocolate cream.

4 Pour the mixture over the croissants, then press them down into the mixture and leave to stand for 1 hour.

5 Preheat the oven to 180°C, 350° F, Gas Mark 4.

6 Place the dish in a deep roasting tin and fill the tin with enough boiling water to come two-thirds up the sides of the dish. Bake for 30–40 minutes or until just set and a bit wobbly. Dust liberally with icing sugar.

Serves 4–6
Preparation time: 20 minutes
Standing time: 1 hour
Cooking time: 35–40 minutes

4 pains au chocolat or
   chocolate croissants
100 g (4 oz) dark chocolate,
   roughly broken into pieces
300 ml (½ pt) milk
568 ml carton double cream
pinch freshly grated nutmeg
4 large egg yolks
170 g tube Carnation
   Condensed Milk
icing sugar, to dust

Chocolate banoffee pie

What can I say about this dessert? It's probably the most famous Carnation Condensed Milk recipe ever. I have updated the classic recipe, making it even more delicious by adding black treacle, mixed spice and dark chocolate.

1 Add the cocoa powder, mixed spice and melted butter to the crushed biscuits and blend well. Press the mixture into the base and part way up the sides of a 20 cm (8 in) spring-form cake tin, then chill well.

2 Make the filling: place the butter and both sugars in a saucepan over a low heat, stirring until the butter has melted and the sugars dissolved. Add the condensed milk and bring gently to the boil, stirring continuously to make a golden caramel. As soon as it comes to the boil, remove from the heat, then add the treacle and melted chocolate and mix thoroughly.

3 Spread the filling over the biscuit base and chill for about 1 hour 30 minutes, until firm.

4 To serve, slice the bananas, fold half of them into the whipped cream and spoon over the toffee base. Decorate with the remaining bananas and dust liberally with cocoa powder.

Serves 8
Preparation time: 20 minutes
Cooking time: 15 minutes

Base

2 tbsp cocoa powder

1 tsp mixed spice

100 g (4 oz) butter, melted

250 g (9 oz) digestive biscuits, finely crushed

Filling

100 g (4 oz) butter

50 g (2 oz) caster sugar

50 g (2 oz) dark brown soft sugar

397 g can Carnation Condensed Milk

1 tbsp black treacle

75 g (3 oz) dark chocolate, melted

Top

4 small bananas

284 ml carton double cream, lightly whipped

cocoa powder, to dust

Stem ginger sponge and sticky orange syrup

Serves 6
Preparation time: 15 minutes
Cooking time: 45 minutes

Sponge

175 g (6 oz) unsalted butter, softened

2 large eggs, beaten

170 g tube Carnation
    Condensed Milk

225 g (8 oz) self raising flour

½ tsp baking powder

75 g (3 oz) stem ginger in
    syrup, finely chopped

Sticky orange syrup

100 g (4 oz) icing sugar

200 ml (7 fl oz) water

pieces of stem ginger, roughly
    chopped

2 tbsp stem ginger syrup

2 tbsp orange jelly
    marmalade, no peel

pared and chopped zest and
    juice of an orange

crème fraîche or custard, to serve

This is a real favourite in our house – I think it's the syrup that makes it a real treat! The kids especially love this pudding. Just as well it's so simple and easy to make.

1 Preheat the oven to 180°C, 350°F, Gas Mark 4.

2 Place all the sponge ingredients, except for the stem ginger, in a large bowl, and whisk until smooth and pale. Fold in the ginger and spoon into a greased 1.4 litre (2½ pt) ovenproof dish. Place the dish in a large roasting tin and fill the tin with enough boiling water to come two-thirds up the sides of the dish. Bake for about 45 minutes until risen and golden brown.

3 Meanwhile, make the syrup. In a small saucepan, bring all the ingredients, except the orange zest, to the boil, and continue to boil for 5–10 minutes until the mixture is slightly thickened. Remove from the heat and stir in the orange zest. Pour the syrup over the warm sponge. Serve with crème fraîche or custard.

Yorkshire rhubarb fool

Serves 4–6
Preparation time: 20 minutes
Cooking time: 10 minutes

675 g (1½ lb) new season rhubarb, washed and cut into 2.5 cm (1 in) pieces

75 g (3 oz) caster sugar

juice of a large lemon

2 tsp vanilla extract

350 ml (12 fl oz) double cream

170 g tube Carnation Condensed Milk

I have always loved the forced rhubarb you get in early January – its subtle flavour and bright pink colour are a real treat in the depths of winter. Having spent time with Janet Oldroyd Hulme in Yorkshire, one of our biggest rhubarb growers, I really appreciate the effort that goes into producing such a uniquely British ingredient. Pay homage to one of our island's finest ingredients with this simple, delicious dessert.

1 Cook the rhubarb in a stainless steel or non-stick saucepan with the sugar, lemon juice and 1 tsp vanilla extract until the rhubarb is softened, thick and pulpy. Allow to cool completely.

2 Whisk together the cream, condensed milk and remaining vanilla to form soft peaks. Gently ripple the cooled rhubarb into the cream, making swirls of bright pink rhubarb in the creamy mixture. Delicious.

Banana, rum and walnut tea loaf

This is the cake we eat at teatime, when the kids come home from school, or on a wintry Sunday afternoon. It really is simplicity itself to prepare and cook, combining old favourites like dates and walnuts with a generous slug of rum. The result is a moist, richly moreish cake.

1 Preheat the oven to 170°C, 325°F, Gas Mark 3.

2 Grease and base line a 900 g (2 lb) loaf tin with baking parchment.

3 Place the dates in a small bowl along with the lemon zest and juice, bicarbonate of soda and 2 tbsp boiling water. Stir well and leave to cool, then add the bananas and rum.

4 In a large bowl, whisk together the butter, sugar and condensed milk until smooth. Gradually mix in the eggs, then the banana, rum and date mixture. Sift over the flour and baking powder and then mix in. Reserve a small handful of the walnuts and stir the remainder into the cake mixture.

5 Transfer the cake mix to the prepared tin, sprinkle over the reserved walnuts and bake for about 1 hour 15 minutes or until a skewer comes out clean when inserted into the middle of the cake.

6 Leave in the tin to cool for about 15 minutes, then turn out onto a wire rack. Delicious spread with butter.

Serves 8
Preparation time: 20 minutes
Baking time: 1 hour 15 minutes

150 g (5 oz) stoned dates, roughly chopped

finely grated zest and juice of a lemon

1 tsp bicarbonate of soda

2 medium bananas (approx. 150 g/5 oz), lightly mashed with a fork

1 tbsp dark rum

75 g (3 oz) butter

50 g (2 oz) dark brown soft sugar

170 g tube Carnation Condensed Milk

2 large eggs, beaten

225 g (8 oz) self raising flour

1 tsp baking powder

100 g (4 oz) walnut pieces

Baked rice pudding with Marsala poached plums

Serves 4–6
Preparation time: 15 minutes
Cooking time: 1 hour

For the rice pudding

200 g (7 oz) Carnation
    Condensed Milk

142 ml carton double cream, plus
    extra (optional) for serving

500 ml (17 fl oz) water

100 g (4 oz) pudding rice

1 vanilla pod

For the plums

150 ml ($\frac{1}{4}$ pt) Marsala wine

1 tsp arrowroot mixed with
    1 tsp water

150 ml ($\frac{1}{4}$ pt) water

25 g (1 oz) caster sugar

9 plums, halved and stoned

2 cinnamon sticks

When I was a child, we always used to have condensed milk in rice pudding. Its creamy taste and syrupy texture really makes this classic comfort pudding. All you need then are a few poached plums, livened up with a little spice.

1 Preheat the oven to 180°C, 350°F, Gas Mark 4.

2 Mix together the condensed milk, cream and water in a large jug. Rinse the rice well, then place in a large saucepan with the milk and cream mixture. Split the vanilla pod lengthways, scrape out the seeds with a knife and add them to the saucepan. Bring to the boil, reduce the heat and simmer for 10 minutes, stirring occasionally. Transfer the rice mixture to a 1.1 litre (2 pt) ovenproof dish, cover with foil and bake in the oven for 40–50 minutes until the rice is cooked.

3 For the plums, mix together the Marsala, arrowroot, water and sugar. Place the plums in a large ovenproof dish and pour over the Marsala mixture. Add the cinnamon sticks and poach, uncovered, in the oven for about 40 minutes until the rice pudding is done. Turn the plums once during cooking.

4 Remove the rice pudding from the oven; it will continue to thicken on standing. If you want to be really indulgent, stir in a few extra spoonfuls of cream when it comes out of the oven.

5 Serve up a generous helping of rice pudding with the warm plums.

Carnation lemon drench cake

This idea came from my mum, who has cooked a wickedly moist lemon cake for years. The secret to its success lies in soaking the cake all the way through with the sticky syrup. Finish it off with a stylish icing.

1 Preheat the oven to 180°C, 350°F, Gas Mark 4.

2 Grease and base line a 20 cm (8 in) spring-form cake tin with baking parchment.

3 Place all the cake ingredients in a large bowl and beat together using an electric hand whisk until just smooth and pale. Pour into the prepared tin and bake for 55–65 minutes or until a skewer comes out clean when inserted into the middle of the cake.

4 Make the syrup by warming together the lemon juice and icing sugar. Whilst the cake is still warm, make holes all over it with a skewer, then gradually spoon over the syrup, allowing it to sink into the cake. Leave to cool in the tin.

5 Make the icing: add the lemon juice gradually to the icing sugar until you have a thick pouring consistency. When the cake is cool, transfer to a serving plate and drizzle over the lemon icing.

Serves 10–12
Preparation time: 20 minutes
Baking time: 55–65 minutes

Cake

225 g (8 oz) butter, softened
4 large eggs, beaten
397 g can Carnation Condensed Milk
50 g (2 oz) ground almonds
finely grated zest and
  juice of a lemon
225 g (8 oz) self-raising flour
1 tsp baking powder
1 tbsp poppy seeds

Syrup

juice of 3 large lemons
100 g (4 oz) icing sugar

Icing

2 tbsp lemon juice
100 g (4 oz) icing sugar, sifted

Posh puds

Marzipan creams

Serves 6
Preparation time: 20 minutes
Cooking time: 20 minutes
Chilling time: 1–2 hours

170 g tube Carnation
    Condensed Milk

150 ml (¼ pt) milk

200 g (7 oz) natural colour
    marzipan, cut into small cubes

5 large egg yolks

25 g (1 oz) caster sugar

2 leaves gelatine, soaked in
    plenty of cold water

2 tbsp Amaretto liqueur

284 ml carton double cream,
    lightly whipped

50 g (2 oz) toasted flaked almonds

maple syrup or honey, to drizzle

Marzipan makes a great mousse. I know it's unusual, but it really works well, topped with a few toasted nuts and a drizzle of maple syrup or honey to set the whole thing off. A few warm English strawberries make a great alternative accompaniment in Summer.

1 Place the condensed milk, milk and marzipan in a saucepan and warm over a low heat, stirring continuously until the marzipan has completely melted.

2 Whisk together the egg yolks and sugar in a large bowl until light and fluffy. Pour the marzipan mixture onto the eggs and whisk well. Pour the mixture back into the saucepan and cook gently over a low heat, stirring continuously until thickened, taking care not to overcook.

3 Drain the gelatine, squeezing out all the excess water. Add to the hot marzipan custard, along with the Amaretto, and stir well until dissolved. Pour into a clean bowl.

4 Fill a large bowl with iced water, then sit the bowl containing the mousse mixture inside it.

5 Stir until cold and starting to thicken. Remove from the bowl of iced water and carefully fold in the whipped cream. You should end up with a thick, cold mousse, which is still pourable.

6 Pour or spoon into six small pots, cover with cling film and chill well. When ready to serve, sprinkle over the toasted almonds and drizzle with maple syrup or honey.

Warm raspberries with Savoy sponge fingers

Serves 6–8
Preparation time: 15 minutes
Cooking time: 6–8 minutes

20 sponge fingers

finely grated zest of 2 limes

juice of 4 limes

450 g (1 lb) fresh or frozen
   raspberries, partly thawed

405 g can Carnation
   Condensed Milk Light

150 g carton 0% fat Greek yogurt

1 tbsp dark brown soft sugar, to glaze

A simple pudding is the perfect way to end a rich meal, which must make this light and fragrant dessert the best finale ever. The raspberries must be slightly overripe to exude their lovely juice and give this pudding its fabulous colour.

1 Preheat the grill to its highest setting.

2 Place the sponge fingers in the base of a large flameproof dish and drizzle over half the lime zest and half the juice. Spoon over half the raspberries and crush lightly with a fork.

3 In a small bowl, mix together the condensed milk, Greek yogurt and remaining lime zest and juice. Spoon this mixture over the raspberry layer and finish with the remaining berries. Sprinkle over the sugar and place under the hot grill for about 5 minutes until the raspberries become slightly glazed. Eat straight away, whilst still warm.

Rose petal Eton mess

This classic combination is the perfect summer lunch or supper pudding. The secret is not to overstir the mixture when combining all the ingredients, so you see the beautiful colours and textures. The best part is the rose petal syrup – the rose flavour works beautifully with ripe summer strawberries. Always pick roses when the weather is sunny, and after the dew has evaporated, to guarantee the most wonderful perfume.

1 Pick the rose petals from the stalks. Roughly chop, place in a small bowl with the rosewater, lemon juice and icing sugar, and leave for 1 hour, stirring occasionally.

2 Using a hand blender, whizz the mixture to a loose purée, leaving small pieces of rose petal visible.

3 In a large bowl, fold together the condensed milk, vanilla extract and whipping cream, then gently fold in the strawberries.

4 Place a layer of crushed meringue in the bottom of a large glass bowl or in six individual glasses. Spoon over a little of the strawberry cream mixture, followed by a little rose petal purée. Repeat the layers, finishing with crushed meringues.

Serves 6
Preparation time: 15 minutes
Standing time: 1 hour

2 (pink) roses, perfumed if possible

1 tbsp rosewater

juice of 2 lemons

3 tbsp icing sugar

200 g (7 oz) Carnation Condensed Milk Light

few drops of vanilla extract

450 ml (¾ pt) whipping cream, lightly whipped

400 g (14 oz) English strawberries, hulled and cut into quarters

6 small meringues or meringue nests, crushed, but not too small

Vanilla blancmange with saffron syrup

Serves 8
Preparation time: 15 minutes
Cooking time: 10 minutes
Chilling time: 1 hour

Blancmange

397 g can Carnation Condensed Milk

300 ml (½ pt) water

1 vanilla pod

4 gelatine leaves, soaked in plenty of cold water

284 ml carton whipping cream, lightly whipped

Saffron syrup

200 g (7 oz) caster sugar

225 ml (8 fl oz) cold water

2 large pinches saffron stamens

juice of a lemon

I once won Chef of the Year with this pudding, it's charming yet unusual. Forget the nasty pink stuff you had at school, this is real blancmange, made properly. I hope you will agree, the results speak for themselves.

1 Pour the condensed milk and water into a large saucepan and mix well. Split the vanilla pod lengthways,scrape out the seeds with a knife and add them to the saucepan. Bring to the boil, stirring occasionally, then remove from the heat. Drain the gelatine, squeezing out all the excess water, and stir into the hot milk. Pour the mixture into a bowl, set aside to cool, then refrigerate for about 45 minutes until it starts to thicken. Gently fold in the whipped cream, then pour into eight 150 ml (¼ pt) Dariole moulds or pudding basins. Chill for 1 hour.

2 Meanwhile, prepare the saffron syrup. Place the sugar, water and saffron in a saucepan and bring to the boil, reduce slightly, then remove from the heat to cool. Add the lemon juice.

3 Dip the moulds in hot water, turn out onto plates, and pour over the syrup.

Decadent chocolate and raspberry torte

For me, bitter chocolate and raspberries are a truly great combination. They work so well together. This pudding is so easy to make, can be made well in advance, and looks really impressive. Go on, forget that diet, just this once!

1 In a small bowl, combine the crushed biscuits and the melted butter, then press over the base of a 20 cm (8 in) spring-form cake tin. Chill well.

2 Place the condensed milk and chocolate in a large bowl. Microwave on high for 1–2 minutes, stirring frequently, until the chocolate has melted. Using an electric hand whisk, beat well until smooth, then leave to cool for a few minutes. Whisk the cream into the chocolate mixture and pour over the chilled biscuit base. Freeze for 4 hours or overnight.

3 To serve, remove from the freezer, run a warm, dry pallette knife around the edges of the torte and remove from the tin. The torte will be super-chilled but not frozen.

4 Pile the raspberries in the centre of the torte and dust liberally with cocoa powder.

Serves 8–10
Preparation time: 20 minutes
Freezing time: 4 hours

Base

150 g (5 oz) double chocolate cookies, crushed

25 g (1 oz) butter, melted

Filling

170 g tube Carnation Condensed Milk

225 g (8 oz) bitter chocolate (70% cocoa solids)

142 ml carton double cream

To finish

225 g (8 oz) fresh raspberries

cocoa powder, to dust

Summer strawberry, mascarpone and coconut cheesecake

Serves 8–10
Preparation time: 25 minutes
Chilling time: 4 hours,
preferably overnight

200 g (7 oz) coconut biscuits, such as
Nice biscuits, crushed
25 g (1 oz) desiccated coconut
75 g (3 oz) butter, melted
405 g can Carnation
Condensed Milk Light
2 x 250 g tubs mascarpone cheese
juice of 2 large lemons
450 g (1 lb) strawberries
2 tbsp strawberry jam

A fantastic summer dessert – the strawberries beneath the cheesecake layer looks stunning when cut, whilst the coconut base adds its own beguiling texture and flavour. Try using blueberries or raspberries instead and you've got three deliciously different puddings in one recipe!

1 Grease and base line a 20 cm (8 in) spring-form tin with baking parchment.

2 Mix together the crushed biscuits, desiccated coconut and melted butter, then lightly press into the base of the tin. Chill.

3 Meanwhile, beat together the condensed milk and mascarpone cheese until completely smooth. Add the lemon juice and combine thoroughly.

4 In a blender or food processor, pulse half the strawberries with the jam until lightly crushed, leaving small pieces.

5 Spread half the cream mixture onto the biscuit base. Spoon over all the crushed strawberries, then top with the remaining cream mixture. Chill for at least 4 hours or overnight.

6 Halve the remaining strawberries and arrange on top of the cheesecake.

Lime and bitter chocolate cheesecake

No desserts book would be complete without a cheesecake. This one is based on the classic American dessert, Key Lime Pie, updated with the addition of bitter chocolate. Really easy to prepare and make, the result is simply stunning.

Serves 8
Preparation time: 20 minutes
Chilling time: 1 hour 10 minutes, preferably overnight

Base

75 g (3 oz) butter
250 g (9 oz) shortbread biscuits, crushed

Filling

2 x 200 g tubs full fat soft cheese
397 g can Carnation Condensed Milk
finely grated zest and juice of 4 limes

To finish

50 g (2 oz) bitter chocolate (70% cocoa solids), melted
8 thin lime slices
50 g (2 oz) icing sugar (optional)

1 In a large saucepan, melt the butter, then stir in the crushed biscuits. Press onto the base of a 23 cm (9 in) lspring-form cake tin. Chill for 10–15 minutes.

2 In a large bowl, whisk together the soft cheese, condensed milk, lime zest and juice for 5 minutes until thick and glossy. Spoon the mixture over the biscuit base and chill for at least 1 hour, preferably overnight.

3 Remove the cheesecake from the tin and place on a serving plate. Drizzle the melted chocolate over the top and sides, then leave to set.

4 To finish, gently simmer the lime slices in a saucepan to which you have added the icing sugar and water – there should be barely enough water to cover the slices. The syrup will reduce to a sticky coating on the limes, and you need to make sure you remove the saucepan from the heat before the lime slices colour or brown. Transfer the lime slices to baking parchment to set before placing on the cheesecake.

Champagne and raisin syllabub

Serves 8
Preparation time: 15 minutes
Chilling time: 1 hour, preferably
overnight

300 ml (½ pt) chilled brut champagne

75 g (3 oz) raisins

**finely grated zest and
    juice of a large lemon**

568 ml carton whipping cream

**200 g (7 oz) Carnation
    Condensed Milk ight**

When I was an apprentice chef, we always had syllabub on the sweet trolley (I'm showing my age now!). This mixture of champagne, lemon and marinated raisins never goes out of style. If you can leave this pudding overnight, it will taste all the better for it. All it needs then are some crisp shortbread biscuits or sponge fingers for dipping. Use inexpensive champagne or sparkling wine; it will make no difference whatsoever to the result.

1 Pour the champagne into a large bowl and add the raisins, lemon zest and juice. Cover and chill for at least 1 hour, preferably overnight, to infuse and plump the raisins.

2 Pour the cream and condensed milk into a large bowl and strain in the champagne, reserving the raisins. Using an electric hand whisk, beat the cream mixture for about 10 minutes until thick and airy. Stir in most of the raisins, reserving some to decorate the top.

3 Spoon into eight small bowls or long stemmed glasses. Top each with lemon zest and a few plump raisins. Chill well, then have some delicate biscuits on hand to dunk into the syllabub.

Peach custard tart with hazelnut brittle

Peach brandy greatly lifts the flavours here, especially if the peaches are slightly underripe. The addition of hazelnut brittle really sets off the flan, not only with its flavour, but also with its contrasting crunchy texture.

1 Preheat the oven to 200°C, 400°F, Gas Mark 6. On a lightly floured surface, roll out the pastry to line a deep 20 cm (8 in) spring-form flan tin, allowing the excess pastry to hang over the sides of the tin. Prick the base with a fork and chill in the refrigerator or freezer for 10 minutes. Cover the pastry base with baking parchment, fill with baking beans, and bake for 10 minutes, then remove the beans and paper and return to the oven for a further 10 minutes. When cool, take a sharp knife and cut away the excess pastry, leaving a neat edge. Reduce the oven temperature to 180°C, 350°F, Gas Mark 4.

2 Place the peaches in a large bowl of boiling water for 30 seconds. Remove and peel away the skins. Arrange the peaches in the pastry case. Heat the cream until nearly boiling. Mix together the egg and egg yolks, condensed milk and brandy. Pour the hot cream onto the egg mixture, whisking continuously, then pour the custard into the pastry case. Bake for about 20 minutes until lightly set: the centre should still be slightly wobbly.

3 Make the hazelnut brittle: place the sugar in a thick bottomed pan and melt over a low heat, stirring occasionally, until caramel brown in colour. Add the hazelnuts, then pour onto baking parchment. Lift the paper carefully, allowing the caramel to run into a thin layer. When cool, snap into shards and scatter over the tart.

Serves 8
Preparation time: 40 minutes
Cooking time: 40–45 minutes
Chilling time: 1 hour 10 minutes

375 g pack ready-made sweet
   dessert pastry
5 ripe peaches, skinned, halved,
   stoned and sliced
142 ml carton double cream
2 large egg yolks
1 large egg
100 g (4 oz) Carnation
   Condensed Milk
2 tbsp brandy (peach brandy
   if you have it)
200 g (7 oz) caster sugar
25 g (1 oz) blanched hazelnuts,
   roasted and chopped

Ice creams
and cold desserts

Highland raspberries and yogurt pots

Serves 4
Preparation time: 10 minutes

50 g (2 oz) porridge oats

500 g tub Greek yogurt

170 g tube Carnation
  Condensed Milk

finely grated zest and juice of a
  lemon

250 g (9 oz) fresh raspberries

1 tbsp runny honey

2 tbsp Scotch whisky

My Scottish chef friend Nick Nairn would say I stole this recipe from him. In my defence, all I can say is that he has 'borrowed' so many of mine over the years, this is payback time! I have enjoyed this pudding with Nick many times, it's a wonderfully light way to end a meal.

1 Place the oats in a frying pan and toast over a medium heat, stirring, until golden. Leave to cool.

2 Mix together the yogurt and condensed milk, add the lemon zest and juice and whip until thickened. Stir in the toasted oats, reserving a few for the top.

3 Crush the raspberries with the honey and the whisky, then gently ripple into the yogurt mixture. Spoon into four serving dishes and sprinkle over the reserved toasted oats.

Mango and banana trifles with mint

Trifle in any shape or form I adore, and this is a lighter version of the classic. I use Carnation Condensed Milk Light instead of custard, and low fat yogurt instead of double cream. Banana and mango lighten things even further.

1 In a large bowl, mix together the condensed milk, Greek yogurt and mint.

2 Place the mango slices and banana in four individual serving glasses. Layer each with a generous spoonful of the yogurt mixture and a sprinkling of biscuits. Serve.

Serves 4
Preparation time: 15 minutes

5 tbsp Carnation Condensed Milk Light

250 g (9 oz) Greek yogurt

8 fresh mint leaves, finely chopped

2 large ripe mangoes, prepared and sliced

2 small ripe bananas, chopped

8 small macaroons or ratafia biscuits, broken into pieces

Banana fudge and cinnamon ice cream

I think the combination of bananas and fudge is a real winner. Eaten on its own, or with fresh fruits, this ice cream is extremely satisfying – and you don't need an ice cream machine to make it.

1 Place the sugar in a thick bottomed saucepan and melt over a low heat, stirring occasionally, until caramel brown in colour.

2 Add the chopped banana and lemon juice and mix well. Cook over a gentle heat for 2–3 minutes, until the caramel and banana softens, then remove from the heat and allow to cool.

3 Mix together the condensed milk, cinnamon and creams, add the caramel banana mixture and stir well.

4 Pour the mixture into a shallow plastic box and freeze until slushy (about 2–3 hours). Beat the mixture with a fork, then stir in the fudge pieces. Freeze again overnight.

Serves 6–8
Preparation time: 15 minutes
Cooking time: 10 minutes
Freezing time: overnight

100 g (4 oz) caster sugar
2 large, firm bananas,
    chopped into small pieces
juice of a large lemon
397 g can Carnation Condensed Milk
2 tsp ground cinnamon
284 ml carton double cream,
    lightly whipped
284 ml carton single cream
200 g (7 oz) fudge, finely chopped

Christmas cake and brandy parfait

Serves 6–8
Preparation time: 15 minutes
Freezing time: overnight

397 g can Carnation Condensed Milk
450 ml (¾ pt) single cream
200 ml carton crème fraîche
1 tbsp vanilla extract
3 tbsp brandy
450g (1 lb) Christmas cake, crumbled
cranberry compote, to finish
   (optional)

This recipe really came about because the kids will not eat Christmas cake or pudding, but, made into an ice cream or parfait, they love it. It's a brilliant way to use up leftover cake or pudding. At other times of the year, any kind of fruit cake will make an excellent substitute.

1 Line a 900 g (2 lb) pudding basin with a double layer of cling film. In a large bowl, whisk together the condensed milk, cream, crème fraîche, vanilla extract and brandy until smooth and creamy. Pour the mixture into a shallow plastic box and freeze until slushy (2–3 hours). Beat with a fork, then stir in the crumbled Christmas cake. Pour into the pudding basin, cover and freeze overnight.

2 When ready to serve, turn out the parfait onto a serving plate and remove the cling film. Accompany with a spoonful of cranberry compote: fresh cranberries simmered until sticky in a syrup of sugar and water.

Strawberry and coconut pancakes

When we had the brasserie, this was one of the bestselling desserts. Most people only serve pancakes on Shrove Tuesday, but this is a brilliant summer pudding. The pancakes can be made well in advance and filled, leaving you to warm them through in the microwave in seconds when you're ready to serve. The orange zest brings out the flavour of the strawberries, just add good quality vanilla ice cream.

1 Make a pastry cream: place the condensed milk and water in a saucepan, mix well and bring to the boil, stirring continuously. Remove from the heat.

2 Whisk the egg yolks until pale and fluffy. Add the sieved flour and mix well.

3 Pour the hot milk onto the egg yolks, whisking continuously. Return the mixture to the saucepan and cook, stirring, over a low heat for 5–8 minutes until thickened. Remove from the heat.

4 Gently heat the coconut in a dry frying pan, stirring occasionally, until toasted to a golden brown. Stir the orange zest and two thirds of the coconut into the pastry cream. Cover with cling film and allow to cool.

5 Place a few strawberries onto each pancake and spoon over some coconut pastry cream. Fold up the base of the pancake by a quarter, then roll up to form a cone. Repeat with all the pancakes and filling, reserving some strawberries. Serve either cold or warm with some more strawberries, the remaining toasted coconut . . . and vanilla ice cream.

Serves 4–8
Preparation time: 20 minutes
Cooking time: 30 minutes

405 g can Carnation
    Condensed Milk Light
150 ml ($\frac{1}{4}$ pt) water
2 large egg yolks
25 g (1 oz) plain flour, sifted
50 g (2 oz) desiccated
    coconut, toasted
finely grated zest of an orange
8 prepared pancakes (French crêpes)
225 g (8 oz) strawberries,
    hulled and chopped

Coffee crème brûlées

Serves 6
Preparation time: 10 minutes
Cooking time: 40 minutes

568 ml carton whipping cream
2 tsp Nescafé Espresso coffee powder
4 large egg yolks
170 g tube Carnation
    Condensed Milk
caster sugar, to glaze

Crème Brûlée comes in all kinds of guises these days, most of which I don't really care for much. Having said that, there's always one exception that disproves the rule and this is it – grown up, sophisticated and truly divine!

1 Preheat the oven to 150°C, 300°F, Gas Mark 2.

2 Place the cream and coffee powder in a saucepan and slowly bring to the boil. Meanwhile, in a large bowl, mix together the egg yolks and condensed milk. Remove the coffee cream from the heat and whisk into the egg yolk mixture. Pour into six ramekins, 7.5 x 4 cm (3 x 1½ in), or similarly sized coffee cups.

3 Carefully place the ramekins in a deep roasting tin and fill the tin with enough boiling water to come two thirds up the sides of the dishes. Cover with foil and bake for 40 minutes until just set. Remove from the oven and place the ramekins on a rack to cool. Chill well.

4 To glaze the brûlées: preheat the grill to its highest setting. Sprinkle a thin layer of caster sugar over each dish, ensuring the custard is covered. Place under the grill for about 5–6 minutes until the sugar has melted to a golden brown. Alternatively, use a cook's blowtorch. Cool slightly before serving.

Caramel parfait

Most recipes require an expensive machine to make perfect ice cream, but not this one! Parfait means 'smooth', and this recipe really is silky smooth and dead simple – trust me, you can't fail. The Munchies make a great addition to the smooth textured parfait.

1 Make the caramel: place the butter and sugars in a non stick saucepan over a low heat, stirring until the butter melts and the sugar dissolves. Add the condensed milk and bring gently to the boil, stirring continuously to make a golden caramel. Carefully stir in half the milk and leave to cool completely.

2 Line a 900 g (2 lb) loaf tin with a double layer of cling film.

3 Whip the cream with the remaining milk until just thickened. Gently fold in the caramel and the chopped Munchies, then pour into the prepared tin. Freeze overnight.

4 To serve, turn out the parfait onto a serving plate. Remove the cling film and cut into slices.

Serves 6–8
Preparation time: 15 minutes
Cooking time: 15 minutes
Freezing time: overnight

100 g (4 oz) butter
50 g (2 oz) caster sugar
50 g (2 oz) dark brown soft sugar
200 g (7 oz) Carnation
    Condensed Milk
150 ml (¼ pt) milk
284 ml carton double cream
2 packets Nestlé Munchies, chopped

Lemon and blackberry custards

I really like simple flavour combinations like this. Late summer blackberries set in a chilled lemony custard really can't be beaten.

1 Place the condensed milk, lemon zest and water in a saucepan, mix well and bring to the boil. Remove from the heat and whisk into the egg yolks. Return the mixture to the pan and cook over a low heat to thicken slightly. Allow to cool a little, then stir in the cream.

2 Arrange the blackberries in the base of four serving pots or cups. Pour the custard over the blackberries to partially cover, then chill well in the refrigerator.

3 Finish with a sprinkle of lemon zest and icing sugar.

Serves 4
Preparation time: 15 minutes
Cooking time: 10 minutes

397 g can Carnation Condensed Milk
finely grated zest of 3 lemons
300 ml (½ pt) water
142 ml carton whipping cream
4 large egg yolks, beaten
250 g (9 oz) fresh blackberries

To serve

chopped zest of a lemon
icing sugar

Tropical meringues with lemon cream

Serves 6–12
Preparation time: 15 minutes
Cooking time: 1–2 hours, plus
drying

Meringue

4 egg whites
225 g (8 oz) caster sugar

Filling

170 g tube Carnation
Condensed Milk
284 ml carton whipping cream
juice of half a lemon
6 passion fruits
200 g (7 oz) fresh pineapple, cut
into small chunks

I love to pair fruit with thick cream and meringue. Along with trifle, it's my favourite combination. Passion fruit and pineapple are slightly tart, so marry well with the sweetness of the meringue. Kiwi fruit also works very well, chopped into small chunks.

1 Preheat the oven to 150°C, 300°F, Gas Mark 2. Line two large baking sheets with baking parchment.

2 In a large bowl, whisk the egg whites with an electric hand whisk until stiff peaks form. Gradually whisk in the caster sugar, one tablespoon at a time, whisking on a fast speed until the mixture is glossy. Place a heaped tablespoon of the mixture onto the prepared baking sheet and mould into a nest shape. Repeat to make 12 nests, spacing them well apart. Place in the oven, immediately reducing the temperature to 140°C, 275°F, Gas Mark 1, and bake for 30 minutes. Turn off the oven and leave for 4 hours or overnight to dry out.

3 Whip together the condensed milk and cream until thick, then stir in the lemon juice. Divide the mixture evenly between the meringues. Scoop the seeds and flesh from the passion fruit into a bowl and add the pineapple chunks. Spoon the fruit onto the meringues.

Sweets and treats

Pecan pie

This classic American dessert is another great favourite of mine.
I find the original version too sweet, so I have adjusted my version
accordingly. That said, I always serve my pecan pie with clotted
cream and vanilla ice cream . . . I know, I know!

1 For the base, preheat the oven to 200°C, 400°F, Gas Mark 6. On a lightly
floured surface, roll out the pastry to line a deep 20 cm (8 in) loose bottomed
fluted flan tin, allowing the excess pastry to hang over the sides of the tin.
Prick the base with a fork and chill in the refrigerator or freezer for
10 minutes. Cover the pastry base with a sheet of baking parchment and fill
with baking beans. Bake for 10 minutes, then remove the beans and paper
and return the pastry case to the oven for a further 10 minutes. When cool,
take a sharp knife and cut away the excess pastry, leaving a neat edge.

2 Reduce the oven temperature to 170°C, 325°F, Gas Mark 3.

3 In a large bowl, whisk together all the filling ingredients except the pecan
nuts. Pour into the pastry case, then carefully sprinkle over the pecans. Bake
for about 50 minutes until the filling is just set.

4 Remove from the tin and leave to cool for about 20 minutes. The pie
is at its best either served warm with vanilla ice cream or chilled with
a spoon of crème fraîche.

Serves 8
Preparation time: 20 minutes
Chilling time: 10 minutes
Cooking time: 50 minutes, plus
20 minutes for the pastry

Base

375 g pack ready made
   shortcrust pastry

Filling

3 large eggs, beaten
150 g (5 oz) dark brown soft sugar
2 tbsp golden syrup or maple syrup
170 g tube Carnation
   Condensed Milk
100 g (4 oz) butter, softened
1 tsp vanilla extract
150 g (5 oz) pecan nuts

Blueberry mallow rocky road

Let the purists sneer, but I love Rocky Road with a large cappuccino. It's so homely and satisfying.

1 Place the chocolate, condensed milk and butter in a large bowl. Microwave on high for 1–2 minutes, stirring frequently until the chocolate has melted. Beat until smooth and then stir in the brazil nuts, blueberries and finally the marshmallows. Spread the mixture onto a baking sheet lined with baking parchment.

2 Melt the white chocolate in a microwave for 30 seconds to 1 minute. Drizzle over the top of the rocky road, leave to set, then break into pieces.

Makes 16
Preparation time: 10 minutes
Cooking time: 2 minutes

200 g (7 oz) dark chocolate, chopped

200 g (7 oz) Carnation
   Condensed Milk

25 g (1 oz) butter

100 g (4 oz) brazil nuts,
   roughly chopped

75 g (3 oz) dried blueberries

200 g (7 oz) mini marshmallows

75 g (3 oz) white chocolate

Hazelnut and chocolate chunk cookies

Makes about 30
Preparation time: 10 minutes
Cooking time: 15–18 minutes

225 g (8 oz) unsalted butter, softened

225 g (8 oz) caster sugar

170 g tube Carnation
   Condensed Milk

350 g (12 oz) self raising flour, sifted

100 g (4 oz) dark chocolate, chopped

100 g (4 oz) hazelnuts, roasted,
   chopped

I used to cook mini versions of these biscuits for petit fours when I was head chef at the Castle Hotel in Taunton – they really are that good. Even better, the mixture can be made raw, and frozen, then cut and baked when you want fresh biscuits.

1 In a large bowl, cream the butter and sugar until pale. Stir in the condensed milk. Mix in the flour and then work in the chocolate and the nuts. Divide the dough in half and place each half in a square of foil or cling film. Roll into two thick sausage shapes. Chill well; this dough will keep quite happily in the refrigerator for a week or so.

2 When ready to bake, preheat the oven to 180°C, 350°F, Gas Mark 4.

3 Peel off the cling film or foil, cut off thick slices, and batch bake in the oven on trays lined with baking parchment for about 15 minutes or until golden brown at the edges, but still a little soft.

Caramel cakes

Caramel in any form is very nice, but here it's combined with white chocolate to make a wonderful cake slice. My mother used to cook something similar when we were kids, and it always went down a treat.

1 Line a 20 cm (8 in) square brownie tin with baking parchment.

2 To make the base, process the biscuits until they are like crumbs, then stir in the melted butter. Spoon this mixture into the tin and, very lightly, press to make an even layer. Chill for 20 minutes.

3 Place the butter and sugar in a non stick saucepan over a low heat, and stir until the butter melts and the sugar dissolves. Add the condensed milk and bring gently to the boil, stirring continuously, to make a golden caramel. As soon as it comes to the boil, remove from the heat and leave to cool slightly.

4 Spoon the caramel over the crumb base in an even layer. Pour the melted white chocolate over the caramel, spreading it out to the edges.

5 When the chocolate has hardened a little, but before it has set hard, cut into slices, and enjoy with a cup of coffee.

Makes 16 pieces
Preparation time: 10 minutes
Chilling time: 45 minutes

For the base

200 g (7 oz) butter shortbread biscuits
50 g (2 oz) butter, melted

For the filling

150 g (5 oz) butter
150 g (5 oz) dark brown soft sugar
397 g can Carnation Condensed Milk

For the topping

250 g (9 oz) white chocolate, melted

Cherry berry fruit bars

Makes 12
Preparation time: 15 minutes
Cooking time: 25–30 minutes

150 g (5 oz) butter
50 g (2 oz) dark brown soft sugar
397 g can Carnation Condensed Milk
1 tbsp golden syrup
250 g (9 oz) porridge oats
100 g (4 oz) dried cranberries and
   cherries
250 g (9 oz) ready-to-eat
   apricots, sliced
75 g (3oz) pumpkin seeds
75 g (3 oz) sunflower seeds

Great lunch box food for the kids, even better for adults. These chewy bars are studded with good things. Just mix all the ingredients together and bake.

1 Preheat the oven to 180°C, 350°F, Gas Mark 4.

2 Line an 18 x 28 cm (8 x 11 in) baking tin with baking parchment.

3 In a large saucepan, melt the butter and sugar together over a low heat. Add the condensed milk and golden syrup. Remove from the heat and stir in the oats, the dried cranberries and cherries, the apricots and 50 g (2 oz) each of the pumpkin and sunflower seeds. Press into the prepared tin, then lightly press on the remaining seeds. Bake for 25–30 minutes until golden. Allow to cool, then cut into 12 bars.

Sticky toffee raisin and rice squares

Fun lunch box or party food is worth its weight in gold. When I whip up a batch of these, I even get the kids to lend a hand with stirring the mixture. They love it, fighting over who gets to lick the bowl.

1 Grease and line a 20 cm (8 in) square tin.

2 In a large, non stick saucepan, melt the butter and sugars over a low heat until the sugar has completely dissolved, stirring continuously. Add the condensed milk and golden syrup and gently bring to the boil, stirring. Simmer for exactly 1 minute, then stir in the raisins and puffed rice. Pour into the prepared tin and leave to set in a cool place. When cool, cut into squares.

Makes 16
Preparation time: 10 minutes
Cooking time: 10 minutes

100 g (4 oz) butter
100 g (4 oz) caster sugar
75 g (3 oz) dark brown soft sugar
397 g can Carnation Condensed Milk
3 tbsp golden syrup
100 g (4 oz) raisins
75 g (3 oz) crisp puffed rice

Citrus drizzle pancakes

Serves 4
Preparation time: 10 minutes
Cooking time: 20 minutes

225 g (8 oz) plain flour

1 tbsp baking powder

pinch of salt

4 tbsp Carnation Condensed Milk
  Light, plus extra to drizzle

2 large eggs, beaten

25 g (1 oz) butter, melted

300 ml (½ pt) milk

oil for frying

2 pink grapefruits, peeled, pith
  removed and cut into segments

2 oranges, peeled, pith removed and
  cut into segments

Fruity, American-style pancakes stacked with juicy citrus slices are simple, yet look impressive. You can use the pancakes straight from the pan, or make them well ahead and reheat.

1 Sift the flour with the baking powder and salt into a large bowl and make a well in the centre. Pour the condensed milk, eggs and melted butter into the well with a little of the milk. Beat together with an electric hand whisk until smooth, then gradually add the remaining milk.

2 Heat a little oil in a large frying pan over a moderate heat. Ladle enough batter (about 4 tbsp) into the frying pan to make small, puffed up pancakes, and cook for about 1 minute, then flip over and fry for a further minute on the other side until golden and risen. Repeat to make 12 pancakes.

3 Layer the warm pancakes with the citrus segments and generous drizzles of condensed milk.

Ginger and cherry fudge

One of the few things I haven't mastered over my many years as a chef is the art of making good fudge. I freely confess, therefore, that this fail-safe recipe was perfected not by me, but by Carnation's very own domestic goddess. She always makes me look good, believe me.

1 Grease and base line a 20 cm (8 in) square cake tin with baking parchment.

2 Heat the milks, sugar and butter in a large, non stick saucepan over a low heat, stirring until the sugar dissolves completely. Bring to the boil and simmer over a low heat for 10–15 minutes, stirring continuously and scraping the base of the pan, until a soft ball of fudge is formed when a little of the mixture is dropped into a jug of ice cold water.

3 Remove from the heat and beat the fudge by hand until thick and grainy (about 10 minutes).

4 Gently stir in the remaining ingredients. Pour into the prepared tin and leave to cool before cutting into squares.

Makes approx. 1 kg (2¼ lb)
Preparation time: 20 minutes
Cooking time: 20–25 minutes

397 g can Carnation Condensed Milk
150 ml (¼ pt) milk
450 g (1 lb) demerara sugar
100 g (4 oz) butter
150 g (5 oz) glacé cherries, halved
50 g (2 oz) stem ginger, chopped

Bitter chocolate and orange truffles

Makes 30–35
Preparation time: 10 minutes
Cooking time: 10 minutes
Chilling time: 4 hours, preferably overnight

200 g (7oz) bitter chocolate (70% cocoa solids), broken into pieces
300 g (11 oz) Carnation Condensed Milk
3 tbsp whipping cream
2 tbsp orange liqueur
finely grated zest of a large orange
cocoa powder, to dust

This is the simplest way to make home-made truffles. They can be prepared well in advance and stored in the refrigerator – all you need to do is dust with a little cocoa powder just before you serve coffee.

1 Put the chocolate, condensed milk and cream in a large bowl. Place in the microwave and heat on high for 2–3 minutes, stirring occasionally until the chocolate has melted. The mixture will thicken quite a lot – this is normal. Mix in the orange liqueur and zest. Cover and chill for 4 hours, or overnight, so the chocolate sets really well.

2 Line a large baking sheet with baking parchment and coat it liberally with cocoa powder. Using a teaspoon, scoop the mixture into truffles, then drop onto the cocoa powder and coat well. Lift out, place on a baking sheet and chill well in the refrigerator.

Index